After the Others

BRUCE WEIGL

poems

After the Others

TRIQUARTERLY BOOKS
NORTHWESTERN UNIVERSITY PRESS

Evanston, Illinois

TriQuarterly Books
Northwestern University Press
www.nupress.northwestern.edu

Printed in the United States of America

10 9 8 7 6 5 4 3 2

ISBN 978-0-8101-5091-1 (cloth)
ISBN 978-0-8101-5092-8 (paper)

Library of Congress Cataloging-in-Publication Data

Weigl, Bruce, 1949–
    After the others : poems / Bruce Weigl.
        p.   cm.
    ISBN 0-8101-5091-3 (cloth : alk. paper). — ISBN
    0-8101-5092-1 (pbk. : alk. paper)
        I. Title.
    PS3573.E3835A69 1999
    811'.54—dc21   98-54631
                                                        CIP

in memory of Denise Levertov

The world was all before them, where to choose
Thir place of rest, and Providence thir guide:
They hand in hand wandring steps and slow
Through Eden took their solitarie way

John Milton

Contents

Part Two
Our Eden

Acknowledgments

Grateful acknowledgment, along with my appreciation for their generous support, is due to the editors of the magazines in which these poems first appeared:

American Poetry Review: "And we came home," "Ant," "On Not Finding Frost's Grave in the Dark," "A Brief Ontology," "The Future," "Errata," and "Elegy for Matthews."

Harvard Review: "Elegy for Her Whose Name You Don't Know."

Kenyon Review: "The Singing and the Dancing," "Praise Wound Dirt Skin Sky," and "The Inexplicable Abandonment of Habit in Eclipse."

The Ohio Review: "Anniversary of Myself."

Press: "The Happy Land."

The Progressive: "Our Independence Day."

Quarterly West: "Cult of the Car."

Rafters: "The Latin for Black Widow," and "In the Realm of Cricket."

Salt Hill Journal: "Why I Hate Theory."

Shenandoah: "For the Anthropologist, Merging," "Our Lies and Their Beauty," and "Morning at Ca Lu River."

Solo: "Elegy for Her Whose Name You Don't Know" "Gambling," and "Lost in LA."

The Southern Review: "Pineapple."

TriQuarterly: "After the others," "What He Said When They Made Him Tell Them Everything," "The Choosing of Mozart's *Fantasie* Over Suicide," and "River Journal."

I am most grateful for the help and support of my family and of my friends who read and scrutinized many of these poems with a much needed and clear-headed rigor, including Andrew and Jean Weigl, Toby Thompson, Mule Hass, Kevin Bowen, and especially Reg Gibbons, and with gratitude for the support of Ellen Levine and David Bonanno.

After the Others

Part One

 Providence

After the others

everything changed.
They took the mountains
then crossed the river
swiftly in their long boats.
Always they have come.
They took the trees.
They took the brown earth

and the small houses.
They silenced the voices
and took the words
so no one could tell the story
of the time before
because they have always come,
because there is no time before.

Under a single blue cloud
a man and a woman touched each other.
An unfaithful gratuity of dogs appeared.
The old people stopped speaking.
They would not bear witness
to the visitations
or to the jangled, rising noise of gabble

conjured in place of a history. God
was invented
        so they could bear their suffering.
In the end
        they had only each other
and wandering, alone,
        that was not enough.

Ant

I saw the proverbial ant,
load of dead moth flesh
across its back, stumbling,
but purposeful to the exquisite,
headed home
along its trail of sweat and tears.

I was not looking for meaning.
I wanted only to ease myself
away from our earth
into nothing
and I saw my own stunned white body
slung across the ant's back
as it trudged towards the dark inside
and the hum of our good news.

The Happy Land

I dread those lace doilies
        lonely women stitch
for the ill,

and the surplice of the unchaste
        boy who serves the morning mass,
though always

I have believed and practiced prayer,
        even when I stalked those alleys
to murder in mindless boyhood boredom

so many righteous songbirds
        that I will never know their forgiveness
which I had imagined

would feel like their tiny hearts felt
        sputtering out in my hand because
I had launched those jagged stones so precisely.

Praise Wound Dirt Skin Sky

Praise wound.
Praise dirt in the wound
that made the metal
fester in the skin.
Praise wound
that closed over
like night sky.
Praise the sharp
cutting metal
exploded into splinters,
physics of shrapnel,
my science.
Praise skin,
how it pushed
the splinters out
against all odds
through the scar
to the cot
in the city
where I waited
where I walked
in the place of emperors.

In the Realm of Cricket

Because he is the last cricket alive
 in the glass world my son built for his lizards,
this one begins to sing
 with his luminous saw-blade legs.

On the forked branch we cut from a spruce,
 the lizards sleep on top of each other
and blink as though they each
 had discovered a star to cling to.

Their bellies full,
 they do not hear or care
for the cricket's song
 that seems a clear announcement against time.

From under the only rock,
 the last cricket tells its story.
How all the others,
 whose names we may not say because they're lost,

have gone before.
 How they left neither in anger, nor with regret.
How the world is no less without them,
 which is why he must sing.

The Inexplicable Abandonment of
Habit in Eclipse

My father and his father
punched the card in and out every day
and did not love their lives.
They worked too hard for nothing wages,

then bitched to their wives in restless beds
and grew around themselves
a coat of sullenness.
I was not conscience-calmed then.

Almost always I played a silent war game to myself,
and a memory of my father
leaning in the doorway
watching night birds

sweep and then
pass upwards
into a suddenly dark afternoon sky
gives me no peace.

Prologue in Minor Key, for the Ancestors

They thought the sun was a wheel,
    turning,
and in their great horror
    they imagined that it would stop.

Now blood runs in our rivers,
    while we loved
and we loveless ones
    linger in the gauzy field of time

that we invented,
    that we believe
does not circle the sun
    or make the sun circle itself.

We live inside of a history
    that no longer remembers us,
that began when the sky was torn through
    with someone's red

fingers at the heights of their sacred places
    that rose from the river valley
where our people cut out living hearts
    to feed to the sun, to keep it moving.

What He Said When They Made Him Tell Them Everything

Bad coke blues. The way some people
    feel the music more.

The way the music
    comes inside and takes their bodies

(I have seen this happen),
    and takes their arms and legs and hips. The hips

are especially taken.
    She came from the other life

to show me her face
    and to open herself

so I could taste the world
    blessed once more

and once more damned.
    And how I squatted that way in Cholon

the hour before light
    so the cruising MP's

would think I was not who I was,
and I would lift us all

to be among the lilies
piled high as men if I could.

Her face so close to mine, so soon and public
made me shiver

in the memory of her
by the river of the green place

where we had been torn apart.
I felt her hard bite on my arm

that could have been harder,
angel's blood in my mouth

in the inn by the circle of afternoon
boys where she lay into my curled shape. I

wanted to note the passage of loss through our bodies:
the azaleas that would blossom into nothing,

that would not forgive the winter its indiscretions;
the red bud mouths that would not open in time.

The Latin for Black Widow

Not the hummed vibration
    through her body's
trailing silk

at his blind and selfish
    moves inside her realm,
she most desires the wait before the kill;

the mating,
    knowing what will follow undeniably after.
Then she cleans herself,

and she does what looks like
    preening for the no one there.
Then she puts her house back into tidy order.

The Idea of Form at Spruce Creek

Brown trout thick as forearms
quiver themselves

cool in what current's left
of late summer drift.

For nerve-twitched mayflies
to float precisely overhead,

they wait,
or they won't eat at all.

No heavy spring snow this year,
no soaking rain for weeks.

The creek is low
so even in their deepest

pools I see the speckled
light of fin and pulsing gill.

All morning long I watch one,
suspended alone and careful,

      until the osprey
comes before I hear its shriek

      or hollow-wing-bone dive.
It's the trout who tells me

      that the hawk is near,
when under dark and weedy cutbank

      I see it flash
until the hungry, white wings disappear.

To Adrian from Crow

Crow in a low branch
of a bare tree
means go easy
on your bloody soul,

as does a single crow
walking in small circles
in a newly turned field.
Two crows

cawing songs
low down
in their selves
means trouble with a woman.

Crow eating a nestling robin
fallen to the bright street
means a new order.
Raucous crow

calling loudly
from nowhere
only once
means someone's lost.

Wanting Again

I listened to the rain
because I needed to find the words
    I had lost somehow

in a tussle with the evil ones
    in a dusty, timeless square of light.
I wanted the rain

    on the new trees and thirsty flowers
to tell me a story
    that could save my soul

from this spiraling
    to a place empty of words.
All night it has rained

    on these new summer trees,
on these blood-red azaleas,
    thirsty as children.

Elegy for Her
Whose Name You Don't Know

She only felt your heart
beat on her sex is all, but still
you can't bear how alone we are,
so before the nothing,
on the lotus path,
you pause to consider
what light you would stand in
for the thousand lives.

We learn this by letting go. We learn this
from moonlight fallen wild on the still pond.
In the grass of her grave you find sense.
In the green grass,
grown to the shape of her body.

Errata

In the olive groves Jesus had lingered
so long after Mary had come
to fetch him to heal her feverish brother
that Lazarus, believing,
died in the tearing garden sun.

Never mind that Lazarus
did not want to return;
the impatient, irresistible Christ
raised him to his feet
as if by a chord of nervous light,

and left him standing there, amazed
in his death stench, beheld. And later,
grieving, he could not drink
or make praise with the others,
rejoicing. He did not know how to be.

He waited for a sign
that he knew would never come
until beyond the hubbub,
he disappeared through a seam
where even the Christ could not go.

The Before

When the man and the woman
    were taken by the angel
to the eastern gate,

they had not yet invented the world.
    They had not yet made up the blues,
or the devil. They kissed the violets

because the violets waited,
    while Michael, in his sorrow,
tried to make for them a panorama,

a history
    unfolding from that single moment
outwards into time.   Michael

tried to show them their undoing.
    Lost in providence,
rivers were waiting to be named.

The man and the woman
    must have heard the world's music,
they must have cleaved

to that human din
     as if to a god,
but they could not have known

how great their loss,
     how righteous
their cloaks of sin.

River Journal

I keep a wall of rock or trees
      to my back. My eyes will always find a way
that's safe

because I've always feared what's underneath things.
      Naked river. Devout river.
Implacable river that touches itself.

I wanted to stand in the river one late evening
      storm. Some of the spirits told me   Go back.
Some of the spirits called me

to their company in deep water.
      Dark living shapes slid past, wind
too warm for the hour.

Such a soaking rain this evening, lord.
      All the little cities I'd held in my hands,
washed away.

Anniversary of Myself

A lifetime ago

I squatted down on a curb
in a frozen twilight parking lot

some fucking where

and looked up into the near
apartment's windows
and at the lives going on
behind them in the light.

The fingers of my gloves had holes.
I don't know what I was doing.
There had been a war
and my people
had grown disenchanted.

I had a fifth of somebody's
whiskey in my pocket. That night
the liquor kept me warm.   Now

I flitter branch to branch outside your window,
lit with a thousand watts of something
I can taste and feel but cannot see.

I am moth wing in summer sky.
I am night bird not blinded or butchered
by your unkempt, sleepless dogs.

For the Anthropologist, Merging

She wanted to make the violins
    playing over the blue water
go away.
    In that life I'm on a staircase

in a stranger's house,
    lost happily
among other strangers
    who shake hips to smoky music. Nervous,

the room I look down into,
    and some white stuff up the nose   I'm in
somewhere, Vermont,
    her face like a flower

among the dull unhappy dancers,
    and what we remember,
I love and I hate, but tonight, graciously,
    my daughter

writes the words
    Muá Cam
on a scrap of paper
    at the table of our just finished supper.

She wants to teach me a poem
        in her language, which I love,
and in that light, her hair
        fallen that way, away from her face,

river of her eyes running deep,
        you are recalled to me
clear as the oranges.
        Muá Cam,

season of oranges.
        From root to tip
the sugarcane will be sweet.
        The winds begin to howl.

Why I'm Not Afraid

To be afraid of the wrong and of the cruel
    is to make them more real than they are.
What the takers want to take they can have.

They can have the name
    and they can have the face.
They can have the cheap suit

and the sweet wine.
    They can have the lawn and the garden
furniture. They can have the future

where they must smuggle
    their tiny selves of a self
into the lives of others

to have any life at all. I won't
    let them have the words.
They cannot take the words

or the seamless music of words,
    and with no false tears
can they bless or curse words

into stubborn human shapes
         against the corruption
of their minds and of their historic elms.

The tunnels of goodness
         that we may pass through
they make thick and grim

with the weight of their bodies;
         flesh that isn't flesh,
blood that doesn't know

the river's name.
         They can have the flesh.
They can have the hands

and their rings.
         They can have the offices
of the nothing that they inhabit

like the newly dead.
         They can have the history
that will not

remember for them
         what grace may do
for the sharp

and for the flicking tongue.
     They can have the tongue.
They can have the lips

that I know they have watched
     across the room in their
spiteful reckless longing

for the light inside of us.
     They can have the light.
They can have the chill

and the silence of their
     own pale shadows
that won't work anymore.

Part Two

Our Eden

With mazy error under pendent shades
Ran nectar . . .

John Milton

And we came home

    to the bloody village,
to whole streets of loss,
    whole rooms,
saying what passed for prayer

    because we did not know
how to live in the new world,
    and I would take you,
who are my rose inside me blossoming,

    back to where the sidewalks
are so wide for promenade,
    what the French abandoned,
like their mistresses

    and their architecture
haunted by the savage rule of class,
    gentlemen who'd hanged their brothers
in the doorways of another time.

    We could walk down Nguyen Du Street
beside the lake,
    then follow the lost trolley tracks
back to old Hanoi

and find the seven ancient gates
to save at least their memory. No one
understands how we felt.
Kill it all. Kill it all.

The Choosing of Mozart's *Fantasie*
Over Suicide

The great music I watched
    find its way
through a broken boy's world
    of walls and walls.
I swear to Christ

I never knew for sure if this could be. We say,
    We tried it all but nothing works,
not even when you give
    your heart held out in open hands. We say,
We almost lost him once or twice,

yet never did we cleave that way before.
    And he cleaved too.
He loved the music deep somewhere inside himself
    and found the peaceful thing
the sometimes mad man left behind

between the ache of melody
    and melody undone, and brave
he let himself come back to us
    and never mind that other boy
he'd thought he had to be.

Why I Hate Theory

Kill the others is a theory.
(Someone's name was Charity.)

We are the better ones
is a theory.

We are stronger, smarter,
Whiter. (Take the doors

down from all the rooms
so the girl can't hide is a theory.)

She is pale as water. She is water.
She is water is a theory.

Pineapple

In the white light midnight stop 'n' shop
    a woman asked me
how to choose the pineapple

best for eating right away, that night.
    She said she liked to suck
the juice; her lips were full

and puckered into smile.
    She held one in her hands
like the head of a garroted man

and squeezed with her thumbs
    where the eyes would be.
Towards me

she thrust the syrup prickly leaves
    until they twitched just inches from my face.
I lied and said I didn't know.

Some black hair fell across her face;
    her eyes so comely
for the simple moment's needs,

her shirt unbuttoned low
    so I could see
the slope of breasts

she wanted me to see
    when she bowed her pineapple bow.
I smelled another world on her,

that scent I'd want to breathe and eat too much
    the way we do. I walked away.
I lied and said I didn't know.

Lost in LA

Tiffany loves to rock and roll; she drinks
most rough boys under the night, then sways
her loose hips in a loathsome dance. I think
there's not enough of anything for her, the way
she lives; not love enough, or booze, or food
to keep her satisfied, or light
that could confirm a goodness still resides
inside of us and her, instead of easy spite.

Across her breast she says she wears
an *X* the way the other woman wore the *A*
but *X* means nothing more, she swears,
than nothing left on earth she could adore.
There's not enough of anything, the way
she lives. There's not enough to make her stay.

The Nothing Redemption

Some men's voices rose and fell far away.
       Time changed. Time got
stupid and I stood in line with the gobs,
our drawers at our feet
       so our cheeks we could pull apart.

One boy's
       hole was plastered
closed with his own dried months of shit,
       and the doctor
called a second doctor in,

and the sergeants feigning aimlessness arrived.
       Oh la the boy sang
to the doctors who giggled
       like men when they dream about war.
I could not have imagined

that a man would shit himself
       and let his own shit
dry himself closed.
       I didn't know that you could do that
so they would not take you

into the state;
　　so they would not make you
cross through the door of lies
　　into the greenery's mist.
All night that night I rode out

on a slow train with my cousin,
　　and drunk, I pissed
from the upper berth
　　down onto him
passed out in the berth below.

He never woke up
　　so I thought I should wash him
soapy clean for the killing
　　that I didn't know waited
for us like a bloody

handkerchief,
　　snagged in the bushes,
found by the beast
　　who joins in the search
for the slaughtered.

Cult of the Car

They were on a gorgeous
freeway in America
when somebody wanted a blow job,
him or her,

it doesn't matter
this near the millennium.
Sun slashed this way and that.
Ours is a loveless time
someone thought.

Whoever got it
made a noise,
allegro maestro
like the noise the bull makes
when the matador
is permitted
to honor the light with its blood.

Gambling

When you win you're unconnected
to the force of need that pulls men down.
When the cards feel so suspicious,
so delicious in your hands,
do not think that you can rise
above the other nowhere men
to a kind and garish sun.
Beyond the winning payoff pass of dollars
through those smallest windows
waits the ache of cash inside your pocket,
ill-begotten weight against your heart.

A Foreign Policy

Hunger makes the bellies of the poor
distended like you've seen in photographs,
or maybe in your arms you've held a soul
who hurts like that, in every cell
a wrath that feeds itself the life it may
not ever have except to waste and rend
it into dust. A clawing pang that burns
inside and stalks, no matter where you hide,
no peace. And trucks of food the many great
republics send, can't find their way along
the village roads, to reach the hungry,
waiting in their hungry lives
until the trucks return at last
back to the discontent abundance needs.

Meditation at Las Cruces after a Day with a Friend Who Sometimes Thinks She Is Fire

All through the afternoon
while leaves have lost their color,
she sings out loud about the cloud again,

how it will blossom like a bloody
flower we can't stop watching.
The fire-fall of leaves scatters, impatient

and with such little care for us,
like the minutes we pretend to own.
She watches her children

run from tree to tree,
hiding in a game,
safe for now among the atoms

before the burning begins
deep in the cells,
the haywire untangling of nerves,

and only when the shadows
join their long fingers
can she step away

from the anarchy of afternoons
she can't take back no matter what,
and into what time we have left.

Morning at Ca Lu River

Through triple-canopy jungle
no proper light would pass,
    except the light of bodies
ascending
    to the river of peace we pretended

lingered somewhere above us.
    It did not linger. For those
torn by their bright and bloody
    nails from the world,
it did not linger like that.

The Singing and the Dancing

I found a hole in the stall in the public toilet
    at the university where I work. Four inches across,

the sharp metal
    looked like it had been torn and peeled back in a rage.

From where I sat to do my chore
    the hole was almost level with my eyes.

For looking in? Out? Like you
    I have a greater need for love

of any kind,
    so I imagined the man

cutting and tearing
    and bending back

the metal toilet wall
    to make a human hole,

and I almost see the penis come,
    a shy and hungry thing.

In what looks like a rage,
    a hole was torn into the wall

between toilets
    so men could do

a kind of loving
    on this, our river of two minds.

For the Man with the Snare of the Devil in His Heart

A man told me that on the street before the Friend's School,
     on a hill in the sun, two cars
crashed in a slash of flesh and scalp

so you could hear the metal moan.
     Many parents waited in their cars
for their children who descended

in a wave from their school down the hill. Parts of engines
     still spinning and grinding, the parents panicked,
but their children formed a circle without speaking,

joined hands then bowed their heads.
     Because this man was
weary of carrying so much anger,

he wanted something
     brave to pass between us,
so he gave me the gift of the story.

He wanted to save himself as well.
     In his arms he had carried dying children
through fire and rockets, so their faces

in his dreams had turned him
     violently inwards
for what's come to be his life,

and after the circle of children
     had brought their calm and grace
to the wreckage, they opened their hands.

A Brief Ontology

A bird that I don't even know
comes to the willow
and against the dark rolling in
he sings the one sweet song
he knows will call another song
back to him through the trees.

We watch the neon moon
come up on its track.
To love's door the moon comes first,
hungry and ubiquitous,
the way the purpose of nights like this
is to try to save a thing inside of us
that we keep otherwise trying to kill
with our lives, like with a hammer.

On Not Finding Frost's Grave in the Dark

So close I felt a rift in the air
of the kind when a soul tries to call
but I could not go to his grave.
I'd had enough with the dead,
so I drank something sweet and bitter
among beautiful women
and their stories no one wanted to hear,
and I danced with a boy named Mohammed
in the meadow, angels,
whom I could not distinguish from our bodies,
cutting through what
fleshy light they could find.

Elegy for Matthews

The best long flight
I saw you sleek through,
late summer,
late evening in Penn Station,
the white
Casablanca suit
I'd seen you wear
that same morning,
splattered now with your blood.
I watched you too long
for the sake of goodness,
or for the sake of
even the most simple
kind of grace
we may manage.
I watched you
across the station
move your hips
to the funky music
from a box
some kid rested
on his shoulder,

your formerly
impeccable suit
covered with your dried
and your drying blood.
What hasn't been lost to me,
even now,
is the way that you
walked through that hubbub
after our eyes had met
across the distance between us,
stride of the fox maybe, or maybe
stride of the clever dog,
until you were right there,
before me,
where I felt the generous
light of you again.

I asked your bloody suit
what had happened
with my eyes,
and without a moment's
hesitation
you said you'd just auditioned
for a part

in a Brian DePalma movie,
and then you
smiled that way you did
inside the place that exists
between the kiss
and the last breath
where you had loved
to dwell.
When you told me
the story of your bleeding,
I did not want to take you
up in my arms
and make it stop.
I wanted to run away.

Our Independence Day

I didn't know our night
trees could feel this safe,
three A.M., an early dove

coos for someone;
stars and more stars.
I didn't know

what I didn't know.
I didn't want
a life of anything then, only

a life.
Someone told me,
Let it go, boy,

let the green
untangle from your body . . .
We used to say

It don't mean nothing
over bodies we'd find in muddy battle.
We used to say

God and Mummy in our half-sleep
between red glare
rockets roaring in.   Here,

the night trees feel safe;
at least no human beings
luminous in the sultry garden.

The Future

At last there are too many histories,
    so the daylilies'
unforgiving of late spring

means only
    that the cold
snapped some buds in the night

and has nothing to do
    with our little lives.
We have come to worship the word

for its measure and for its commerce
    and so we have forgotten
much that we had learned

in the old way of reckless
    flight and woeful prayer,
and we have lost

our wild need to make believe.
    But in our denials, exquisitely,
we are accomplished,

and we have learned
        how to teach this to others. Yet tonight
I almost feel in my brain

this summer's soaking rain
        all through these late flowers
as if they were growing inside of me,

a thing we could not account for, here.
        We would say,
It's only rain in the world

and not in our hearts,
        only flowers of our given names
who have no use for us.

Morning of What Would Become the Evening of the Seven Irises .

Forty years ago
a little girl named Belinda MacNamara
whom I loved in the second grade
took me to her house after school.
Under the monkey bars boys fought on
to be like men at recess
she marched up to me
the way she would march later
when she played "MacNamara's Band"
on her record player, in her pink room.
That's my song she would say.
I'm Belinda MacNamara's Band.
She marched up to me
through a cloud of playground dust
and looked hard into my eyes
that Friday of my becoming,
her own blue eyes the color of a still pond.
You're coming to my house today she said.
My mother made cookies. I have a slide.
I have a record player in my own room.
Bells rang in the Boone School across the street
saving me, calling us back
to our stories. I didn't know then
that some things happen only once.

Drinking Song

Stupidly, I said to myself out loud,
    It's time for the cruelty to stop.
I was not thinking about the mountain

worn away by a single stroke of the silk cloth
    every day across the millennia.
I was thinking about the smell of blood.

Later, on the television,
    a handsome woman
posed for the camera, a dangerously

long and thick boa constrictor
    wrapped around her mostly naked body.
I flipped through the channels of floods,

of earth cracking open,
    and the various cleansings.
I think I'll go down the road

and sing my crying song to myself.
    I have heard that the wine
is not so made of water there.

The happiness of others

is not like the music I hear
    after sex

with my wife of the decades
    my wife

of the ocean night grass
    my wife

of the milk heavy
    mother breasts

drowsily dipping towards me
    my wife my rope my bread

Our Lies and Their Beauty

I have loved most
        the inconcruous,
the wildly pointless,

the oddly non-self
        aggrandizing;
how one sweet man

whose mouth I would still kiss,
        lied to me
that his ne'er-do-well father

stood once,
        alone out on a thin steel beam,
dangled

twenty stories
        above the teeming city
by a nervous crane.

The man that he lied was his father
        wears a white muscle T-shirt
in the photograph,

his black hair is curly
      and tangled
nicely in that high city wind

and he smiles a fearlessness
      that you want to but
can't quite believe.

One sad night,
      my friend showed me
the bent-up photograph

of this man on a beam,
      and I did not tell him
how I'd seen it on postcards

many times before.
      It could have been his father.
They were just then building the Waldorf.

My friend lied
      because he wanted his father
to be the man up there in his lie,

and because he wanted to weave something
    frightened that he saw inside of me
with something

that he saw inside of himself,
    the beauty
that must never always be the lie.

Notes

The quotation of the last four lines of Milton's *Paradise Lost* is meant to serve as a preface to this collection. After spending a summer reading long passages of Milton's great poem (I could never read it all), it occurred to me that what follows those lines is the inevitability of our deliverance into the twentieth century and its end. This is especially clear if you consider the passage from book 4 in which the archangel Michael tries to describe for Adam and Eve the enormous consequences of their sin as they stand at the threshold of the eastern gate. "Thus thou hast seen one World begin and end," Michael says, and, "henceforth what is to com I will relate." Soon they will be alone, he wants to tell them; soon they will be sent out to invent the world, but at that moment, they can only stand in wonder at "where to choose/Thir place of rest, and Providence thir guide." I love most how sweetly human this poem is for the way that Milton saw the paradox within the loss of paradise. "We may no longer stay: go, waken Eve," Michael tells Adam, and he does, and the three descend the hill. It must have been soon they looked back and saw their paradise "Wav'd over by that flaming Brand, the Gate / With dreadful Faces throng'd and fierie Armes." What Milton helps us to understand is that in return for this loss of Edenic vision, they are given themselves and, for the first time, a world connected to their lives. This collection is in part an attempt to follow the wanderings of our parents of that "first disobedience" from the moment they stepped through the gate into irony, as well as a record of my discovery of how they have become us, and how we have become them.

I am grateful for the many kindnesses and the support of my friend Laura Knoppers, especially for her patience with my tedious questions about Milton and for the clear light of understanding she brings to his difficult poem.

In the poem "After the others" I have shamelessly paraphrased passages from Milton's *Paradise Lost*, especially from book 20. (Writing a poem while visiting the tomb of Burns, Keats wrote, "I sin against thy native skies.")

"To Adrian from Crow" is for Adrian Lewis, in admiration for his poems.

"Why I'm Not Afraid" is for Tim O'Brien.

The quotation that serves to introduce part 2 is from Milton's *Paradise Lost*, book 4, line 240.

For the poem "On Not Finding Frost's Grave in the Dark," I am grateful to Liam Rector.

For the poem "What He Said When They Made Him Tell Them Everything," I am grateful to C. Rose.

"Morning at the Ca Lu River" is for Larry Heinemann.

"Our Independence Day" was inspired by a conversation with and is dedicated to Charlie Simic.

"The Idea of Form at Spring Creek" is for Harry Humes, who fishes well and lovely.

"Drinking Song" is for FW.

"Our Lies and Their Beauty" is for Duke Moffi.